William D. Chipley

Pensacola

The Naples of America - and its surroundings illustrated

William D. Chipley

Pensacola
The Naples of America - and its surroundings illustrated

ISBN/EAN: 9783337193577

Printed in Europe, USA, Canada, Australia, Japan

Cover: Foto ©Andreas Hilbeck / pixelio.de

More available books at **www.hansebooks.com**

A NEW LIGHT ON FLORIDA.

PENSACOLA,

(THE NAPLES OF AMERICA)

AND ITS

Surroundings Illustrated

SEPT. 1877.

NEW ORLEANS, MOBILE

AND THE

RESORTS OF THE GULF COAST.

BY

W. D. CHIPLEY,

GENERAL MANAGER PENSACOLA R.R.

PENSACOLA

(THE NAPLES OF AMERICA.)

AND ITS

SURROUNDINGS ILLUSTRATED.

U. S. CUSTOM HOUSE AND POSTOFFICE, PENSACOLA.

NEW ORLEANS. MOBILE,

AND

THE RESORTS OF THE GULF COAST.

COMPILED BY W. D. CHIPLEY,

General Manager Pensacola R. R.

BY REQUEST OF THE CONVENTION OF APRIL EIGHTEENTH.

PUBLISHED FOR FREE DISTRIBUTION.

COURIER-JOURNAL PRESS, LOUISVILLE.

MAP OF PENSACOLA, ITS BAY, AND SURROUNDINGS. 1877.

FLORIDA.

"THE AIR BREATHES UPON US HERE MOST SWEETLY."

HOW TO GET THERE.

FORT BARRANCAS.

OFTEN with the tourist, still more frequently with the pleasure-seeker, and always with the invalid or emigrant, the question, *"How shall I get there,"* is of the first importance, not being secondary to the destination. It seems, then, entirely appropriate to give first the best route to Florida, and tell afterwards of the soft, balmy atmosphere, and the attractions for the sportsman with rod or gun. Travelers from Pittsburg and Cleveland, and west thereof, find their shortest line to Jacksonville via Montgomery, Alabama.

Consider these figures:

Montgomery to Jacksonville, ... 425 miles.
Montgomery to Pensacola, ... 163 miles.

Difference in favor of Pensacola, ... 262 miles.

Travelers from all the great Middle and North-western States must go to Montgomery to get to Jacksonville, if they are ticketed by the short line. Arriving at Montgomery, they can reach the Land of Flowers, at Pensacola, within seven (7) hours, against twenty-five (25) hours, the best known time to Jacksonville.

At Pensacola, the resident of a colder and less genial clime will enjoy the most perfect transformation. The senses are rapt by the novelty

3

of the surroundings, the suddenness and entirety of the change. As will be shown later, the traveler will experience, in addition to the charms of climate, attractions and excitements unknown to other parts of Florida.

From the East, passengers will find the distance by the most direct routes as follows:

New York to Jacksonville, ... 1262 miles.
New York to Pensacola, ... 1218 miles.

Difference in favor of Pensacola, ... 44 miles.

With the further difference that Pensacola can be reached by a number of lines, all in *perfect* order, running double daily trains and long lines of sleepers, giving fewer changes than are encountered in reaching any other point in Florida.

PALAFOX STREET WHARF.   (ILLUSTRATIONS FROM PHOTOGRAPHS.)

PENSACOLA.

The splendid Bay of Pensacola, unrivaled for its beauty, depth, and security, was discovered by Panfilo-de-Narvaez, in 1525. Various adventurers gave it different names, as Port-de-Ancluse and St. Mary's Bay, but that of Pensacola, which prevailed, was the true name among the Indians, the natives of the country. The first settlement was made by the Spaniards, in 1686. The first governor was André Arivola, who constructed a small fort, called San Carlos, and erected a church upon the present site of Fort Barrancas. The French took Pensacola in 1719; the Spanish re-took it, and the French again took it in the same year and kept it until 1722, when it was restored to Spain. In the mean time, Pensacola had been removed to the west end of Santa Rosa Island, near the present site of Ft. Pickens, where the Spanish constructed a fort, which afterwards was improved by the English General Haldemand. The settlement remained on the island until 1754, when, the town being partly inundated, the site was removed to the magnificent location which it now occupies. Pensaco-

VIEW OF BAY FROM CENTRAL AVENUE AND SHOT PARK, NAVY YARD.

la was ceded to the English in 1763, by whom it was laid off in regular form in 1765. The town surrendered to the Spanish arms in 1781. On the 7th of November, 1814, General Andrew Jackson, with the American army, entered the town, when the English fleet in the bay destroyed the forts, San Carlos (at Barrancas) and Santa Rosa. Spain recognized "manifest destiny" in 1819, and ceded to the United States the entire territory of Florida. She was admitted into the Union as a State in 1845. During the war between the States, a considerable portion of the old Spanish buildings were destroyed but many still re-

BARRACKS AT FORT BARRANCAS.   (FROM PHOTOGRAPH.)

main, and their quaint appearance strikes the stranger immediately. Since the war Pensacola's advance has been marked. Its population has been more than doubled, and its progress in architecture can be seen by the illustrations in this book. Extensive docks have been constructed, and other improvements accomplished, which stamp Pensacola as a growing city.

THE CITY AND SANTA ROSA HOTELS.   [ILLUSTRATIONS FROM PHOTOGRAPHS.]

PENSACOLA'S COMMERCIAL IMPORTANCE.

As this publication is for the eye of the pleasure-seeker, invalid, tourist and sportsman, but brief mention will be made of Pensacola's commercial importance. Pensacola Bay, spacious enough to accommodate the navies of the world, and deep enough to load and discharge the largest vessel alongside the railroad docks, renders Pensacola's position unrivaled. Its easy access to and from the Gulf, its direct accessibility to and from the Western, North-western, and Central Southern States, must furnish a very large regular and rapidly increasing business in transportation to and from its ports, not only of lumber, but also of cotton, grain, coal, iron, and all the products of the West Indies and South America.

It is but necessary to add Pensacola's Annual Marine Statement for the year ending July 1, 1877, to astonish the uninformed.

Foreign vessels entered. . . .	270,	tonnage	200,801,	men in crew		4,273.
American " " .	. 110,	"	35,560,	"	"	987.
Coasting " " .	. . 210,	"	59,208,	"	"	2,198.
Total vessels	590,	"	295,569,	"	"	7,458.

The value of Exports from Pensacola during the same year amounted to $2,291,822.

MARINE TERMINUS PENSACOLA RAILROAD. (ILLUSTRATIONS FROM PHOTOGRAPHS.)

Consider 7,458 men coming to Pensacola each year from every quarter of the Globe, the 1,200 stevedores and assistants who make Pensacola their winter home, and its resident population of 6,000, and it can truly be said that Pensacola offers more stir, variety, and reality of life than any city in Florida. What port in the State, or in America, can show over 200 square rigged vessels in its harbor at one time, as is often the case at Pensacola? This attraction will steadily enhance, as arrangements are being perfected to export iron and coal in increased quantities, via Pensacola; and cotton and grain shippers have at last awakened to the remarkable facilities that are offered by the port, and the exportation of both has been fairly started.

CLIMATE, HEALTH, SOCIETY, CHURCHES, SCHOOLS.

Florida has been called the Italy of America, and the thousands who have breathed its genial, healthy, life-giving atmosphere will cheerfully testify that it is no misnomer. In summer the heat is tempered by a gulf breeze of softness and purity unsurpassed, and the thermometer seldom reaches 92°. Dr. J. C. Whiting, from thermometrical observations at his hospital, in Pensacola, gives the following table of mean temperature for 1876:

January.	54.71
February	54.56
March	64.98
April.	62.93
May	75.40
June	81.00
July	84.55
August	84.10
September	81.44
October.	71.34
November.	58.89
December.	49.60

The "Indian Summer" of the Middle and more Northern States closely resembles a Florida winter, and will convey a better idea than can be written of a season which in Florida admits of life in the open air, while citizens of

A. STODDARD'S RESIDENCE.   (FROM PHOTOGRAPH.)

the North are hovering
over great fires or shiv-
ering in heavy wraps, as
the rude blasts of winter
cut to the bone. The
fact that the thermom-
eter rarely falls below
32° fits Pensacola as a
grand sanitarium for the
whole country. Three
times within twenty-five
years yellow fever has
scourged Pensacola, but
in every instance the ep-
idemic was traceable to
some ship from an infect-
ed port. In no instance
has the disease ever orig-
inated in the city, nor
does it ever extend into

RESIDENCE OF COMMANDANT AT NAVY YARD.

the country beyond the city limits. A proper quarantine always protects
the city, and in 1875 it kept Pensacola free from fever, even when it was
raging at the navy yard, where it was carried by a marine who surrepti-
tiously visited an infected vessel for the purpose of trading.

Liability to yellow fever being controlled, Pensacola's baths, boating,
and fishing are rapidly increasing its popularity as a summer resort. Winter
and summer its healthfulness is marvelous, except during epidemics. To
winter visitors the fever is of no concern, as it is gone before they come.
They luxuriate in a soft, salubrious atmosphere, with health in every
breath. All classes of chronic diseases, such as diarrhea, dysentery,
rheumatism, diseases of the kidneys, and incipient pulmonary cases are
benefited and relieved by a visit to Pensacola.

Invalids in the advanced stages of phthysis pulmonalis who have visited
St. Augustine have experienced the too stimulating effect of the salt air.
This class will find the same difficulty at Pensacola, with this difference
and advantage: They can remove into the interior, and among the piney
woods breathe the salt air of the gulf modified into gentle zephyrs, which
the invalid may safely inhale, and which never fail to re-animate and ben-
efit. At the same time the location is not out of the world, but within less
than twelve hours' journey from the cities of New Orleans, Mobile, Pensacola, and Montgomery. Statistics testify to the healthfulness of Florida.
Notwithstanding the fact that so many thousands of consumptives resort

to the State for relief, the proportion of deaths from pulmonary complaints in it is less than in any other State in the Union. The census of 1870 showed that these deaths were as follows:

Massachusetts . . .	one in 283
Maine	" 315
Vermont	" 463
New York	" 379
Pennsylvania	" 470
Ohio	" 507
California	" 450
Virginia	" 585
Indiana	" 599
Illinois	" 698
Florida	" 1,433

EPISCOPAL CHURCH.

The Presbyterian, Methodist, Episcopal, Baptist, and Catholic congregations have comfortable church buildings. The illustration shows the Episcopal Church the oldest house of worship in the city, having been constructed more than half a century ago. The system of public schools is liberal and efficient, and in addition a number of private schools are well supported. Principal among the charms of Pensacola is its society. The people are pleasant, refined, and intelligent, and the stranger is surprised at the cordial hospitality extended from every quarter.

HUNTING, FISHING, BOATING, BATHING.

By consulting the map of Pensacola and its surroundings, the reader will observe the net-work of water-courses, bays, and bayous centering at that city. The water is clear, bright, and beautiful. Surf bathing upon Santa Rosa beach as enjoyable as language can express, the salt water bathing in the bath-houses of the bay, and bathing in fresh water as clear as crystal, can all be had within a distance of seven miles. One may weary of St. John River, which at first impresses the beholder as grand, but soon becomes monotonous. How different the broad, beautiful Bay of Pensacola! On its rolling waters one can never tire. For lovers of St. John scenery the Santa Rosa Sound offers a magnificent substitute, with Live Oak Plantation skirting its bank on one side, and only Santa Rosa Island, with its narrow strip of soil, between it and the blue waters of the Gulf of Mexico on the other. The Perdido Bay is one of the loveliest sheets of water in the

State, rivaled by the Escambia Bay, with its bluffs and ever-moving fleets. Any attempt to particularize becomes confusing, as the special beauties and attractions of the different bays and bayous are remembered. Escambia River is the "Ocklawaha" of West Florida. The stranger who wishes to enjoy a short trip will be pleased as the steamer plows through the broad, placid waters of Escambia Bay, and then delighted with the luxuriance of the tropical growth as the vessel winds its way up the narrow and tortuous channel of Escambia River to Molino. At this point the excursionist can take the train and return by rail to Pensacola.

The fresh water fishing is superb. The waters literally swarm with all kinds of fish, notably trout, black bass, and pike. All varieties of perch abound, including a special kind, a very game fish, called bream. It is not unusual for a good angler to pull out fifty to sixty of these fish in an hour, weighing from a half to one pound. Both in salt and fresh water fishing is carried on with pleasure and profit the entire year. In the bay and bayous every description of salt water fish abound, and in the season fifty cents will purchase half a dozen Spanish mackerel of the size for which the epicure pays seventy-five cents for one half in the restaurants of New York City. These fish, and the salt water trout, give special excitement to those who love a contest with a very game fish. No one can claim to have seen what fishing is until they have visited the snapper banks off Santa Rosa Island. There the famous red snapper can be caught, two at a time, weighing from five pounds to sixty, as rapidly as the line is thrown in. The limit to the quantity catchable is commensurate with the physical endurance of the catcher. An illustration is here given (from a photograph) of four fish caught by a party in Pensacola Bay. One weighing 214 pounds was drawn out after it was killed by shooting, by Thos. R. Hopkins, No. 194 Fulton st., New York.

SPECIMEN OF PENSACOLA FISH.   (FROM PHOTOGRAPH.)

It is claimed that no one can know the flavor of fresh fish until he has eaten a Pompano, at Pensacola. Pensacola's importance as a fishing point is best described by the true statement that its dealers ship all kinds of fish to Mobile, New Orleans and other points, by the car load. Another very attractive amusement is turtle hunting, on Santa Rosa Island. It is not unusual to find as many as 180 eggs in one nest. From the Junction to Pensacola, all around the city, and opposite it, in Live Oak Plantation, every description of game can be found, in large numbers, including deer, turkeys, and partridges, with an occasional bear. It should impress every one that it is not necessary to exile one's self, and endure all the imaginary pleasures of camp life, to secure the best possible sport with rod and gun; both are within from one to three hours' drive, sail, or walk of the hotels. The splendid duck shooting at the mouths of the rivers, in season, should not be forgotten. Oysters of the finest size and flavor are taken in any quantity wanted. Attention has been turned to planting the bivalve, with fine results. Last winter, Mr Alexander Stoddard, of No. 175 Broadway, set out 750,000 in Bayou Texar, along the water front of his fine estate.

RUINS OF FORT M'RAE, WITH FORT PICKENS IN THE DISTANCE.

This chapter would not be complete without mentioning the facilities for reaching, via Pensacola, St. Andrews' Bay, St. Joseph, Apalachicola, and other famous fishing grounds and hunting fields of the Florida coast.

Wild turkeys are seen between the rails of the Pensacola Railroad, and along its line partridges roam apparently without fear. From its coaches the crack of the rifle can be heard as it brings down a deer. It is when the sportsman tires of this game, and desires an encounter with a bear, wild-cat or panther, that he needs to seek St. Andrews and the contiguous country.

THE VICINITY OF PENSACOLA.

The pleasure of boating at Pensacola is not confined to fishing or idly rolling on the mighty wave, or smoothly plowing the placid waters; but added to these charms are the numerous places in the vicinity to go to. The stranger who may visit it will not wonder at finding first on this list Santa Rosa Island. Upon its beach, mid-day in its overflowing brilliancy, makes the beholder feel as if, according to Milton, "Another morn had risen on mid-noon." The sunset comes with a splendor and glory unknown to more Northern climes. As the ever-moving waves roll, with permeated and ever-varying colors, upon the snow-white sand, one feels the awful supremacy of the Almighty, and the littleness of man, in a manner conveyed by no other sight in nature. While on the island, very few visitors fail to find an interest in collecting shells and sea-beans. Then comes a visit to Fort Pickens; this grand and historic old edifice, though denuded of a portion of the iron dogs of war that used to bay, not "deep mouthed welcome home," but roars of defiance, still possesses a multitude of pleasant and interesting sights and objects that make a visit there both profitable and agreeable.

Across the bay is the Navy Yard, and just west of the Navy Yard is Fort Barrancas. Both are beautiful and will interest the most indifferent. Added to the novelties to be seen, is the delightful society enjoyed by all who know the hospitable and intelligent officers of both the garrisons. Below Barrancas is the Pensacola Light-house, illustrated on the cover of this book from a photograph, and said to be the finest light on the Gulf. Near by is Fort McRae, once familiar with all the "pomp and circumstance of glorious war," but where now the solemn bat reigns supreme, in a silence only broken by the

CENTRAL AVENUE, NAVY YARD.

never-ceasing roll of the mighty ocean, as the wild waves dash upon its once proud walls. Years ago it was built upon a foundation which seemed

as enduring as granite, but the Gulf threatened, and for a time its fall was averted by the construction of an immense sea wall. The rolling waters could not be withstood, and the illustrations will show the condition of its ruined battlements, casemates, ramparts, and posterns, which are now tumbling to decay. It is at McRae that the searcher after shells and other marine treasures is most successful. With the old Spanish fort, the pretty villages of Milton and Bagdad, the LiveOak

RUINS OF FORT M'RAE, WITH LIGHT HOUSE IN THE DISTANCE.

Plantation, bays, bayous, sounds, and rivers, this chapter might be extended indefinitely. Suffice it to say that the visitor at Pensacola must tire of going, seeing, enjoying, long before the list of attractive places to go to have been exhausted.

WEST FLORIDA—ITS LOCATION AND PRODUCTIONS.

West Florida is in no respect an agricultural country at present, for the reason that heretofore the timber interest has absorbed the entire energies of the country. The timber wealth is on the surface, but under the surface lies hidden wealth which is yet to be dug out of the soil. The climate, as explained in a previous chapter, is semi-tropical and devoid of extremes in heat and cold. The country is the best watered in the world, and its healthfulness is as near perfect as that of any section of the Globe. It is only necessary to let its attractions and advantages be known to see in a few years the entire State dotted with happy homes, churches, schools, and villages. Great fertility by virtue of soil the lands of West Florida do not possess, nor can the combination of extreme fertility and health be found in any new country. But vegetation here performs the prodigy once attributed to the chamelion, it lives on air. Let it but obtain a hold in the earth, and an atmosphere which seldom knows a freeze seems to compel it to grow

PRIVATE RESIDENCES, PENSACOLA. (FROM PHOTOGRAPHS.)

and come to bloom and fruitage in the fine yields of the country. Drouths are not usual, but when they occur crops seem to stand them much better than in higher lati-
tudes. The soil gives
a generous return for
all applications of fer-
tilizers. Nothing is
grown in East Florida
north of Melonville,
that will not grow in
West Florida, with the
difference that eligible
land can be bought in
the latter section for
one tenth the prices
charged in the form-
er. The first settlers
in West Florida will
find a large and re-
munerative market at

BLACKWATER (FORMERLY BAGDAD). SIMPSON & CO.'S MILL.

home for their truck and other products; articles now brought from the up-country by the train-load to supply the resident and visiting population. When the home supply has been met, the farmer will find the lines of trans-portation cheap, quick, and reliable, leading to the great Middle and North-western States, where the fruit shipper from Florida will not encounter the disastrous island competition met with in the cities of the East, where East Florida finds its principal markets. The nearer proximity of West Florida to the interior markets, by nearly twenty-four hours express and over thirty-six hours freight train travel, must create a steady and rapid advance in its agricultural interests.

The new-comer will find lands on the railroads for sale, but should other points be preferred it requires but a glance at the map to note how all the rivers, bays, sounds, and bayous, from the Perdido to the Choctawhatchee River, center in Pensacola Bay, making Pensacola their natural business metropolis, to whose market crops can be floated safely and cheaply.

Every description of melon and vegetable, and all the cereals can be grown, and of the latter suitable kinds can be used successfully for green soiling or for winter pasturage, to assist the immense ranges during the months when the grass and cane are least nutritious. It would astonish a "down-country" planter to see the yield of rice upon these uplands; and sugar cane also makes a remunerative return. It is when fruits are consid-ered that the advantages of the country appear pre-eminent. Lands within a stone's throw of the railroad, worth from $2 to $3 per acre, make the finest peach orchards in America, the yield being of superior size and flavor, and the trees are remarkably long lived. Lands for oranges, lemons, and other semi-tropical fruits, unsurpassed by any in the State, can be had at from $5 to $25 per acre, which with similar location in East Florida would cost $50 to $100 per acre, notwithstanding the advantage of transportation is with the cheaper lands. It would be a grave oversight to omit mentioning the prolific pecan tree, the luscious pears and plums and very fair apples which the soil produces.

West Florida seems to be nature's vineyard, so great is the yield of the numerous varieties of grapes. First, the fruit can be sent to supply the early markets of the North, and later, wine can be manufactured. For the latter purpose the scuppernong, which grows to special perfection, is very greatly prized. Lord Raleigh landed in North Carolina, near Newbern, nearly two centuries ago; he there tasted the scuppernong for the first time, from a vine still in existence, which three years ago, it is said, yielded forty-two barrels of wine.

White, in his description of this grape, says: "We consider this very peculiar grape one of the greatest boons to the South. It has very little resemblance to any of the grapes of the other sorts. It is a rampant grower and requires little, if any, cultivation. It blooms from the fifteenth to the last of June, and ripens its fruit in West Florida about the latter part of August. It has no disease in wood, leaf, or fruit, and rarely, if ever, fails to produce a heavy crop. We have never known it to fail. Neither birds nor insects ever attack the fruit. We are credibly informed that a vine of this variety is growing near Mobile, which has produced two hundred and fifty bushels of grapes in a year, and we know that vines ten years old have given and will give thirty bushels per vine. From three to three and a half gallons of juice can be gotten from a bushel of these grapes, according to ripeness. It is the sweetest and most luscious of any grape we

BLUFF SPRINGS MILL.   (FROM PHOTOGRAPH.)

have ever seen or tasted, makes a fine, heavy, high-flavored, fruity wine, and is peculiarly adapted to making foaming wines."

It would run this theme through innumerable pages to dwell upon the luscious strawberries and other delicacies, but, at the risk of being prosy, the fig must not be overlooked. This fruit, so delightful when eaten ripe from the tree, is the best dried fruit known, and is without a parallel as a preserve or pickle. Mr. Alexander Stoddart, of 175 Broadway, New York, has now every known variety (twenty-two) on his place, and in a few years the pickling for market from his place alone will reach a large amount annually. Mr. Stoddart added sixty acres last year to his orange and pecan groves and orchards of peaches and figs. His vineyards and straw-

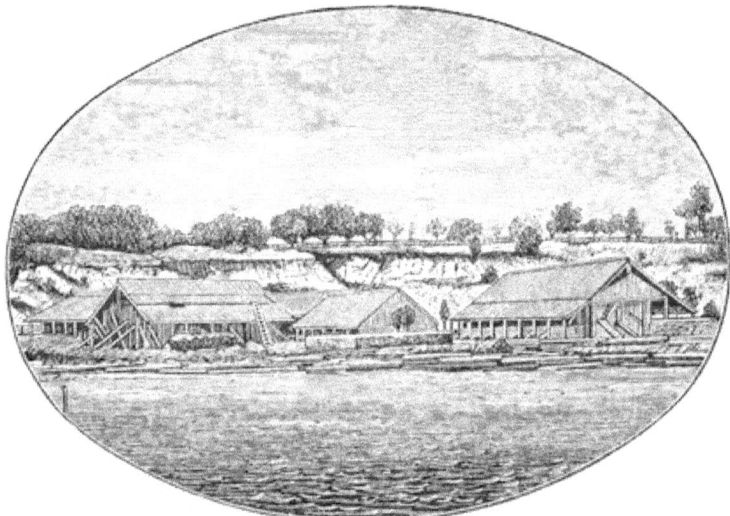

BLUFFS, ESCAMBIA BAY.   (ILLUSTRATIONS FROM PHOTOGRAPHS.)

berry beds have been more than doubled, and in another year he will be running refrigerator cars to the various markets of the North.

The Escambia bluffs shown in illustration above are on the place of the Yniestra Brothers. At this beautiful spot, a veritable Eden, can be found all the products of Florida, including several thousand orange trees. The buildings under the bluff are the sheds under which the bricks for the Dry Tortugas forts were made. These bluffs extend for miles, offering the most desirable location in all Florida for orange groves.

The land is slightly rolling, dry and arable, except occasional swamps near the mouths of rivers and heads of some of the bayous and bays. The rain fall is sufficient, and on the streams, with which the country is so magnificently watered, can be found numerous and superior water-powers.

TURTLE-EGG AND ALLIGATOR HUNTING ON SANTA ROSA.

Santa Rosa Island is a sand key of the Gulf, forty miles long, and varying in breadth from a fifth of a mile to over a mile across; it is the breakwater of Pensacola Harbor, and receives the shock of the rolling seas of the Gulf of Mexico which often break against it in fury, while the waters of the bay within are still as a mill-pond and scarce a ripple washes the beach of the city front seven miles away, though the water at the city is as salt as that in the center of the Gulf. The sea beach of the island is a gently sloping expanse of white sand, back and forth on which the advancing and receding waves will glide for hundreds of feet. You can stand where no water is one moment, and the next be struggling waist deep against a surging wave that is climbing up the strand. This beach is the incubator of the great turtles of the Gulf. Its gradual incline, the easily excavated sand beyond, and the warm southern exposure, adapt it to their approach, the making of nests, and hatching of their eggs. So they resort to it for this purpose, and in due time the young turtles are hatched, unless the eggs are captured by the various creatures, biped and quadruped, who seek them in the season. From Pensacola over to the island is about seven miles, and as the land breeze of the night sets fair across the bay, it is a pleasant trip of moonlight nights to run over on a sail-boat, land on the bay shore, walk across the island, which is not a third of a mile wide opposite the city, and seek for "turtle crawls" on the Gulf beach, or bathe luxuriously in the surf. The "crawl" shows on the sand where the under shell has been dragged along, and following this up to a point above the wash of the highest waves, the nest is found, usually about two and a half feet below the surface. A single nest will contain from 100 to 300 eggs. At Sabine Pass, on Santa Rosa Island, alligators are found by the ten thousand, and are killed in large numbers by hunters who frequent the place.

RESIDENCE OF HON. C. W. JONES, U. S. SENATOR.

PENSACOLA'S TIMBER TRADE.

MUSCOGEE SOUTH MILL.

The immense forests of pitch pine tributary to Pensacola, notwithstanding the large business annually transacted, have as yet only been worked on the edges lying alongside the creeks, rivers, lakes and bayous. Untold acres of virgin forests remain to be stripped of the growth of many centuries, to give place to the farmer, whose labor will make the land smile with a luxuriant wealth of vegetation. This transition must be gradual, and for years to come Pensacola's superior supply, in connection with its absolutely secure harbor and a depth of water which can load a vessel to twenty-three feet within six feet of cars on the railroad docks, must continue it as the chief timber port of the country. The busy whirr of the saw will be heard for at least a quarter of a century before existing forests are gone, and as one growth is cut away another will spring up where the plow of the farmer does not prevent. On the line of the Pensacola Railroad are four mills, two belonging to the Muscogee Lumber Company, the Molino and Bluff Springs, with a cutting capacity of over sixty millions of superficial feet per annum. At Millview, connected with Pensacola by the Pensacola & Perdido Railroad, are six mills, with a capacity of sixty-five millions of superficial feet each twelve months. Simpson's mills, Blackwater, Skinner's, Wright's, Bay Point, Bayou, and others make the aggregate cutting capacity of mills contiguous to Pensacola exceed two hundred million feet per annum. In addition to this sawn stuff, thousands of pieces of hewn timber are floated down the streams to market. Even the forests of the Tombigbee and Alabama rivers have been made tributary to Pensacola, by an arrangement to float the timber to Tensas Station, Alabama, and transport from that point by rail, after it has been loaded by steam machinery. This timber will be discharged at Pensacola into a boom whose capacity exceeds ten thousand sticks. As it is alongside the railroad docks, within the corporate limits of the city, and not more than three hundred feet from water thirty feet deep, the arrangement must give a wonderful impetus to Pensacola's timber trade. It affords absolute security against blows, and avoids the expense and risk of towage from Ferry Pass—in short, it is perfect.

PERDIDO BAY LUMBER COMPANY'S MILL, MILLVIEW. (ILLUSTRATIONS FROM PHOTOGRAPHS.)

ESCAMBIA RIVER SCENERY.

SWEET FLORIDA, GOOD-BYE!

A SONG.

WRITTEN BY MR. DRAKE, CLERK OF MAJ. OGDEN, U. S. ENGINEERS, UPON HIS DEPARTURE FROM FLORIDA.

(Popular in Pensacola thirty years ago.)

Sweet Florida, good-bye to thee!
　Thou land of song and flowers,
Where generous hearts and beauty dwell
　Amid thy fragrant bowers.
The interest deep, the love I feel,
　Bound by each genial tie,
· Bloom like thy sweet magnolia.
　　Sweet Florida, good-bye!
　　Sweet Florida, good-bye!

I go to seek another clime,
　But go where e'er I may,
The love I bear to thee and thine
　No change can chase away.
Santa Rosa's snow-white sands
　Are fading from my sight;
Farewell awhile to thee and thine.
　　Sweet Florida, good-night!
　　Sweet Florida, good-night!

MOBILE, NEW ORLEANS, AND RESORTS OF THE GULF COAST.

MOBILE.

Mobile lies in latitude 30° 41′, at the head of the bay and mouth of the river of the same name. The surrounding country, broken into beautiful undulations, is covered with pine timber, the resinous exhalations from which give such celebrity to this region as conducive to health. These hills and valleys are carpeted all the year with green grass which grows luxuriantly amid the tall pines of the forest.

Mobile possesses peculiar attractions to the seeker after pleasure, comfort, or health. Its climate is mild and salubrious; its inhabitants genial, hospitable, and refined; its residences abound with evidences of a cultivated taste, and here may be seen during the entire winter flowers in full bloom and trees loaded with oranges. Here also the mere seeker after ease may enjoy that comfort denied in a colder and more inhospitable climate, and the more robust may enjoy field sports within easy reach of the city. The bay swarms with fish and ducks. Snipe and woodcock frequent the savannahs of the pine lands, and the rolling hills, rising hundreds of feet, are haunts of the partridge and deer.

WOOLSEY ENTRANCE TO NAVY YARD, PENSACOLA.

The water of all this pine region is peculiarly pure, and its streams are clear and beautiful. The soil is sandy, and consequently, even in wettest weather, there is practical freedom from mud. Fruits and vegetables are grown during the entire year in the open air, while fresh and salt water fish, and game, complete the attractions of the market.

No place affords more delightful drives or smoother roads. The visitor is confined to no special one, though the loveliest of all is the shell road, which leads through groves of magnificent magnolias along the margin of the broad and lovely bay.

This bay lies between many points of interest to the student of history. Near its outlet is Fort Morgan, occupying the site of old Fort Bowyer, which once repelled a large British fleet, and where recently a yet more famous strife took place. Near this and opposite is Fort Gaines, and further on Fort Powell, while at the head of the bay is Spanish Fort. Around all of these many memories cluster. At various contiguous points are mounds erected by an unknown people, and in these mounds are found the remains of these extinct races.

Near the city, on the line of the Mobile & Ohio Railroad, are many healthful resorts, chief among which is Citronelle,

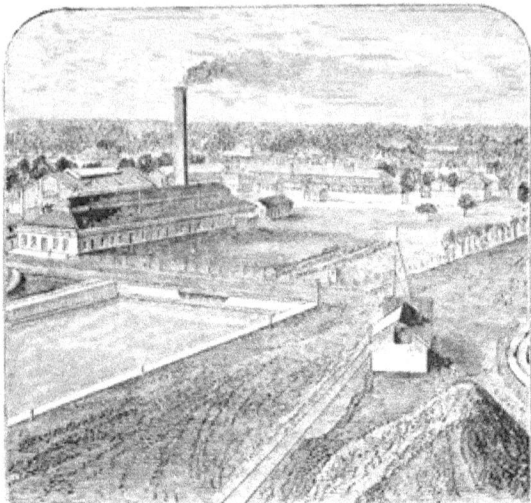

BIRD'S-EYE VIEW OF NAVY YARD, PENSACOLA.

a village rapidly becoming famous for the salubrity of its atmosphere, so peculiarly favorable to those suffering from pulmonary disease. This town is reached by a special accommodation train in addition to the daily mail service. And along the eastern shore of the bay are villages, with cheap and comfortable accommodations for boarders, as far as Point Clear, where

RUINS OF OLD SPANISH FORT NEAR PENSACOLA.

there is a large, commodious, and well-kept hotel, all reached daily by a pleasant trip on a fine low-pressure steamer. From Mobile to New Orleans, distant 140 miles, the railroad skirts the Gulf of Mexico, and all along are villages and cottages where may be combined the peculiar attractions of this coast and all the appliances of civilization—daily mails, telegraphs, and rapid

transit to near and great centers of population.   All this region is expedi-
tiously and pleasantly reached by the Mobile & Ohio R. R., which stretches
out its arms 500 miles northward, and by the Montgomery & Mobile R'y,
extending to Montgomery, with connections to all points west and north,
inviting from colder climes the pleasure seeker, tired man of business, and
invalid, to enjoy themselves and recuperate in its balmy air.

YNIESTRA BLOCK, PENSACOLA.   [FROM PHOTOGRAPH.]

NEW ORLEANS.

New Orleans! How the mere sound comes freighted with visions of
pleasure, luxury and comfort.   The Paris of America it certainly is, but
its delights are not confined to the gayeties of life.   Within its abundant
resources every taste and disposition find their full measure of pleasure
and ease.   It would be a superfluity for these pages to dwell upon the
attractions of this glorious old city, for they would repeat things charming
enough in themselves, but as familiar all over the country as household
words.

The tourist would be well repaid by a visit to this grand old city, filled
with monuments of historic lore.   Here are the famous plains of Chal-
mette, memorable by the rout of the British by Jackson.   Here also Forts
St. Philip and Jackson defending the entrance to the city.

The French Market is a unique feature of New Orleans, with its many varied and attractive stalls laden with every luxury in the shape of game, fruit, vegetables, fish, oranges, etc. One meets representatives of all the nations of the earth, all talking at the same time in their respective tongues, and making a perfect Babel of sounds. This market is celebrated over the entire country for its delightful coffee, and no visitor to the city fails to visit the market for the purpose of trying it.

Numberless lines of city railway cars traverse the principal streets, affording rapid transit from one point of interest to another. The Branch Mint, on Esplanade Street, when in operation, is well worth a visit. A ride on the levee, with its forests of masts and shipping, steamers, flat-boats, and barges which line its side for miles, is novel and pleasant.

The Jockey Club Course, Fair Grounds, and the various cemeteries, monuments, churches, and other public buildings, afford innumerable points of attraction. In fact it would take too much time and space to begin to enumerate the many points of interest or places of amusement, for their name is legion. This city is noted for the hospitality of its people and the beauty and elegance of its women.

Previous to the opening of the New Orleans & Mobile Railroad the attractions of the Gulf Coast of Mississippi, either as a summer or winter resort, were of comparatively local celebrity. The only means of communication was a daily line of steamers, running between New Orleans and Mobile, and stopping at the various points along the coast; and yet thousands of families from the interior of the states adjoining were regular visitors, season after season, while a great many built residences and occupied them permanently. But from the date of the opening of the railroad, and the more rapid, frequent, and convenient communication thus established, the advantages of a sojourn on the the coast became more widely known, and people from all parts of the country came, both as

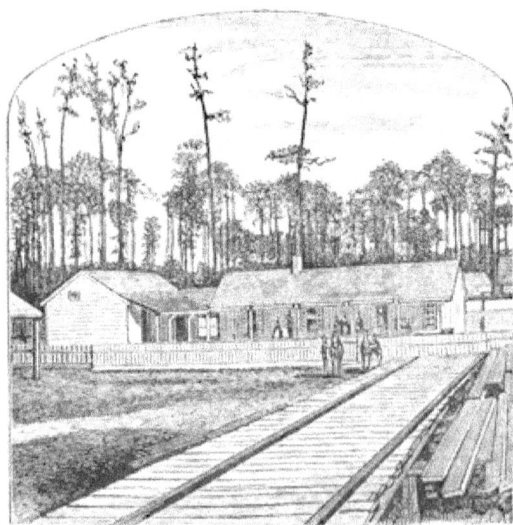

A PINEY WOODS HOME, FLORIDA.   (FROM PHOTOGRAPH.)

summer and winter visitors. Possessing a remarkably mild, pleasant and healthy climate, fanned by the salt day breezes from the Gulf, the shade heat of summer rarely exceeds 85°, and the cold of winter scarcely ever reaches the freezing point. The great abundance of game, fish, and oysters, and the fine sailing, rowing, and bathing, entice the visitor to that healthful out-door recreation which

PENSACOLA & PERDIDO RAILROAD WHARF, PENSACOLA.

makes a sojourn at any of the points along the coast no less enjoyable than beneficial to health.

Beginning at Waveland Station—about forty-five miles from New Orleans—a line of residences, almost unbroken except by the bays and inlets of the coast, extends for nearly fifty miles. Clustering together here and there, by the side of some broad and quiet bay, these seaside homes form themselves into villages, at which the railroad company has established stations, and where the visitor finds hotel or boarding-house accommodations, churches, schools, and all facilities for healthful enjoyment.

A vast pine forest, seventy-five to one hundred miles wide, and reaching almost the whole length of the coast, mingles its balsamic odors with the salt breezes of the Gulf, bringing health to the feeble and pleasure to all. Millions of wild fowl of all descriptions swarm about the bays and marshes during the winter months, and the hunter never fails to bring back abundance of game from his excursions among the neighboring islands.

Oranges of unsurpassed flavor are grown in abundance along the whole coast. Not a residence or hotel that does not have its bearing orange trees, and at various places extensive orchards of this most delicious fruit are to be seen flourishing side by side with the peach, pear, apple, fig, and olive tree. In addition to the attractions of a healthful, mild and equable climate, fully equal in all respects to that of Florida, a short ride over one of the finest and best equipped railroads in the country, takes the visitor sojourning on this coast to New Orleans or Mobile, and thus combines all the pleasures and comforts of city life with those of the winter resort. No traveler, seeking either health or pleasure, will fail to appreciate the advantage of this nearness to the unvarying round of winter amusements for which New Orleans is so justly celebrated.

CONTINENTAL HOTEL, PENSACOLA,   FROM PHOTOGRAPH.

WAVELAND STATION—47 Miles from New Orleans.

At this point the residences on the coast begin, and extend side by side, to the bay of St. Louis. There are as yet no hotels, but several private boarding-houses will accommodate visitors. The soil is well adapted to the culture of almost all fruits and vegetables. Several extensive orange orchards and scuppernong vineyards are now under successful cultivation.

BAY ST. LOUIS—52 Miles from New Orleans.

This thriving village is situated on the western shore of the Bay of St. Louis, and extends around on the Gulf front. There are three very comfortable hotels and many private boarding-houses. Population about 2.000. Episcopal, Presbyterian, Methodist, and Catholic congregations. Two public and several excellent private schools for both sexes. One of the loveliest views in the South is that presented to the traveler approaching Bay St. Louis by the railroad from the east. The broad Bay on the right, and the waters of the Gulf on the left, with the beautiful sweep of the shore, covered with verdure, and crowned with its line of neat white cottages, form a picture of calm and lovely beauty which can not but charm the senses of the traveler seeking rest or health. The railroad company has erected a costly and handsome station-house at this point, where passengers breakfast and dine.

Commencing far up the shore of the Bay, a well kept shell road, eight miles in length, runs along the top of the bluff around the point, and westward on the Gulf shore for several miles, making one of the finest drives in the country. Several large oak groves in the vicinity of the station are being fitted up by the railroad company for picnic grounds.

STREET SCENE, PENSACOLA, WITH RESIDENCE OF LATE HON. S. R. MALLORY, EX-SEC'Y C. S. NAVY, IN CENTER.

PASS CHRISTIAN—58 Miles from New Orleans.

Pass Christian has a permanent population of about 2,000. There are three handsome church edifices: Episcopal, Presbyterian, and Catholic. Three public schools, a fine school for young ladies, and a very excellent private school for boys; also a Catholic institution for small children. Several good hotels and private boarding-houses. Furnished houses can be had at reasonable rates by the month or season. Pass Christian is justly celebrated for the number of handsome residences it contains, and for its fine shell road, extending along the entire water front of the village.

MISSISSIPPI CITY—70 Miles from New Orleans.

Mississippi City is the county seat of Harrison County. It has a permanent population of about 400. Two good hotels—the Tegarden Hotel, situated near the station, and convenient to the water, and Barnes Hotel, directly on the front. Excellent fishing and boating all the year around.

BILOXI—80 Miles from New Orleans.

Biloxi has a permanent population of over 2,100, and is one of the most thriving towns on the coast. It is situated on a peninsula formed by the Back Bay of Biloxi and the Gulf, being thus almost surrounded by fine fishing and ducking ground. Deer Island, a narrow strip of land, a short distance off the front of the town, is a favorite resort for both hunters and fishermen. There are four churches: Methodist, Baptist, Episcopal, and Catholic. Good public schools, and several fine private educational institutions. The Montross House and other fine hotels and boarding-houses offer excellent accommodation to visitors.

MOLINO MILLS, PENSACOLA RAILROAD.

OCEAN SPRINGS—85 Miles from New Orleans.

The situation of Ocean Springs differs from other towns along the coast, in the fact that the land here rises to a greater altitude and is more broken or rolling. On the west it faces the Bay of Biloxi, and on the south the Gulf. At various points in the town and vicinity mineral springs, possessing rare medicinal qualities, are found, the virtues of which were traditional with the Indians who formerly inhabited the coast. The population of the town is about 1,900. There are four churches: Methodist, Baptist, Episcopal, and Catholic. One public school and four private institutions of learning. The Ocean Springs Hotel has been recently purchased by Northern parties, and completely furnished, with a view to the entertainment of Northern visitors. In addition to the fishing, hunting, and boating to be enjoyed at this point, the mineral springs are highly recommended by the medical faculty for the relief of many chronic diseases.

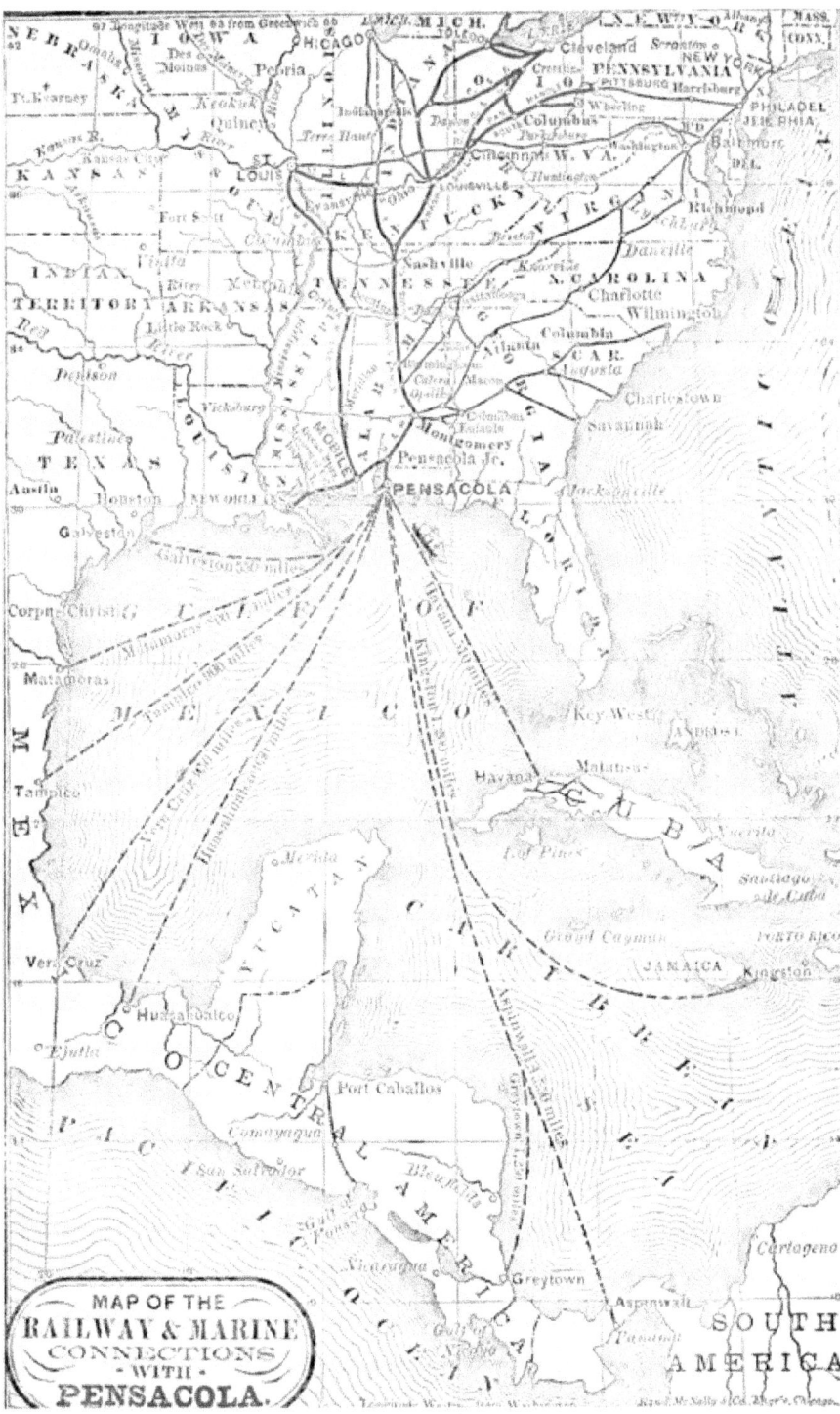

MAP OF THE
RAILWAY & MARINE
CONNECTIONS
- WITH -
PENSACOLA.

MOBILE & OHIO RAILROAD

THE POPULAR LINE BETWEEN

New Orleans, Mobile, Pensacola,

AND ALL POINTS SOUTH AND SOUTHWEST,

AND

CHICAGO

VIA MOBILE AND ST. LOUIS.

THE ONLY LINE RUNNING

PULLMAN PALACE AND SLEEPING CARS

Between St. Louis and New Orleans.

WITHOUT CHANGE.

CONNECTIONS.

At COLUMBUS, KY., with St. Louis, Iron Mountain & Southern Railway.
At UNION CITY, with Nashville, Chattanooga & St. Louis Railway.
At RIVES, with Paducah & Memphis Railroad.
At HUMBOLDT, with Louisville & Nashville & Great Southern Railroad.
At JACKSON, TENN., with Mississippi Central Railroad.
At CORINTH, with Memphis & Charleston Railroad.
At MERIDIAN, with Ala. & Chat., Ala. Cent., and Vicks. & Meridian R. R'ds.
At MOBILE, with New Orleans & Mobile Railroad.
At MOBILE, with Mobile & Montgomery Railway for PENSACOLA.

PASSENGER TRAINS ARE FULLY EQUIPPED WITH

Westinghouse Air Brake and Miller's Safety Platform and Coupler.

Tickets can be obtained via this Route at all

PRINCIPAL TICKET OFFICES IN THE U. S. AND CANADA.

RATES ALWAYS AS LOW AS VIA ANY OTHER LINE.

A. L. RIVES,	C. FLEMING,	CHAS. L. FITCH,
Gen'l Manager.	Ass't Gen'l Sup't.	Gen'l Pass. Agent.

For a Copy of this Book Free send your address to W. D. CHIPLEY, Gen'l Manager P.R.R., Pensacola, Fla

FLORIDA.

The wonderful salubrity of the climate of Florida is destined to make it the refuge of those who seek to escape the rigor of a Northern winter, so that the choice of a route is, of course, the first and most important consideration to those who intend going there. We would, therefore, invite the attention of our friends and patrons to the splendid facilities afforded by the

ST. LOUIS & SOUTHEASTERN RAILWAY.

Being the SHORT LINE between St. Louis and the Southeast, the traveler saves many miles by purchasing his tickets via this popular route.

The St. Louis & Southeastern
RAILWAY,

THE SHORT LINE

And positively the Best Route from

ST. LOUIS TO NASHVILLE, TENN.,

Where it connects for all points

SOUTH AND SOUTHEAST.

INCLUDING

Chattanooga, Atlanta, Augusta, Macon, Brunswick Savannah, Jacksonville, Fla., Charleston, Decatur, Huntsville, Montgomery, Pensacola, Mobile, New Orleans, Bristol, Knoxville, Lynchburg, Petersburg, Norfolk, and Richmond,

THUS FORMING THE

Great Trunk Route between these Points, St. Louis and the Great West.

Travelers, remember this is the PASSENGER AND MAIL ROUTE. It affords you the advantage of

Pullman Palace Sleeping Cars on all Night Trains

Arrangements have been made whereby we are enabled to furnish Tourists with

ROUND-TRIP TICKETS TO PENSACOLA, FLORIDA

AT GREATLY REDUCED RATES.

Also, EMIGRANT TICKETS have been placed on sale by this Line, and special inducements are offered to Colonists and Emigrants.

J. H. WILSON, Gen'l Manager.   JNO. W. MASS, Gen'l Pass. & Ticket Agent.

☞For a Copy of this Book Free send your address to W. D. CHIPLEY, Gen'l Manager P.R.R., Pensacola, Fla.

New Orleans & Mobile Railroad.

NEW ORLEANS

—) AND (—

ALL POINTS IN TEXAS

VIA THE

MOBILE LINE.

NEW ORLEANS, via

Washington, Richmond, or Lynchburg and Atlanta.

THROUGH PULLMAN CARS PHILADELPHIA to NEW ORLEANS WITHOUT CHANGE.

NEW ORLEANS, VIA
CINCINNATI, LOUISVILLE & MOBILE

Through Pullman Cars New York to Cincinnati—Through Pullman Cars Cincinnati to New Orleans.

Passengers via Montgomery can take Pensacola en route, or passengers via Mobile can diverge at that point for a visit to the Bay City.

As an additional feature for the accommodation of Western Travel going South, attention is called to the

THROUGH PULLMAN SLEEPING CAR

Leaving St. Louis daily, at 10 P. M. on the

St. Louis & Iron Mountain, Mobile & Ohio and New Orleans & Mobile Road

Arriving at New Orleans at 11.25 A. M. the second morning.

Connection with this car is made from Eastern Cities, via Chicago or Indianapolis by either of the Great Trunk Lines Westward, without change of Cars.

ALL THE ADVANTAGES OF MODERN TRAVEL

Are thus given to every section of the country over

THE MOBILE LINE!

The equipment of this line "has no equal south of the Ohio River."

The engines are of the first class, and always in perfect order.

The Day Parlor Cars are models of elegance, fully equipped with the Automatic Air Brake, and all conveniences for the toilet.

Elegant Eating-Houses, smooth track, beautiful views and fast time.

S. E. CAREY,	**F. P. MARSH,**	**D. B. ROBINSON,**
G. P. & T. A., New Orleans.	E. P. Agent, New York.	Sup't, New Orleans.

For a Copy of this Book Free send your address to W. D. CHIPLEY, Gen'l Manager P.R.R., Pensacola, Fla.

— THE —

St. Louis, Iron Mountain & Southern

RAILWAY

OFFERS THE BEST ROUTE

From St. Louis

AND ALL POINTS WEST AND NORTHWEST,

— TO —

PENSACOLA

Mobile and New Orleans.

EXPRESS TRAINS

WITH

PULLMAN SLEEPING CARS

TO PRINCIPAL POINTS

Through Without Change.

For Particulars call upon or address E. A. FORD, Gen'l Passenger Agent, St. Louis, Mo.; or

H. H. MARLEY, Northern Pass. Agent, 104 Clark St., Chicago, Ill.

☞ For a Copy of this Book Free send your address to W. D. CHIPLEY, Gen'l Manager P.R.R., Pensacola, Fla.

—THE—
Mobile & Montgomery
—RAILWAY—
IS THE
GREAT THOROUGHFARE
FROM THE
NORTH AND EAST
TO THE
GULF PORTS
AND THE
Cities in Southern and Central Texas.

The longest continuous lines of Sleeping Cars in the world are run over this line, which, on account of its

Natural Position, Rapid Transit and Sure Connections,

Has been awarded the Fast Southern Mail. This line is equipped with all the modern appliances—Westinghouse Automatic Air-Brakes, Miller Platforms, etc.

Consult the latest official Time Tables, AND COMPARE THEM WITH ALL OTHER ROUTES, and see the advantages gained in points of time and seasonable hours of arrival and departure at all principal cities.

EDMUND L. TYLER, Vice-Pres't and Sup't, MONTGOMERY, ALA.

GEO. NASON, Gen. Pass. and Fr't Ag't, MOBILE, ALA.

☞For a Copy of this Book Free send your address to W D. CHIPLEY, Gen'l Manager P.R.R., Pensacola, Fla.

EXCURSION RATES

— TO —

FLORIDA!

THE

Pensacola Railroad

IS THE ONLY LINE

BY WHICH

Florida can be reached with Excursion Tickets

INQUIRE OF TICKET AGENTS EVERYWHERE.

CHEAP HOMES

ON LONG CREDIT.

THE PENSACOLA RAILROAD WILL SELL 80,000 ACRES OF LAND
UPON THE FOLLOWING CONDITIONS:

EVERY ALTERNATE QUARTER SECTION (160 Acres),
OR EVERY ALTERNATE HALF SECTION (320 Acres),

Will be sold to actual settlers who will make improvements, at

- **10 Cents per Acre Cash;**
- **25 Cents per Acre in one year, no interest;**
- **25 Cents per Acre in two years, no interest;**
- **25 Cents per Acre in three years, no interest;**
- **25 Cents per Acre in four years, no interest;**
- **$3 for Cost of Deed.**

Let the many who are looking to Florida as their future home "prospect" in the West, as well as the South and East, before they determine on localities. The Western portion of Florida can well afford to risk the comparison.

For further information, or a copy of this Book *Free*, address

W. D. CHIPLEY, Gen'l Manager, Pensacola, Fla.

"THE PEOPLE'S FAVORITE."

LOUISVILLE & CINCINNATI

SHORT LINE

RAILROAD.

THE QUICKEST, BEST AND ONLY LINE

With which Passengers from the South make direct connection at Louisville with

PULLMAN PALACE SLEEPING CARS

Running through to

Pittsburg, Harrisburg, Philadelphia, New York and other Eastern cities

WITHOUT CHANGE.

This is the Only Line by which Pullman Southern Sleepers are run from New Orleans, Mobile, Jackson, Miss., Montgomery, Grenada, Decatur, Jackson, Tenn., and Nashville to Cincinnati, and from Cincinnati to same points without change.

The Only Line by which Pullman Palace Sleepers are run between Louisville New York and other Eastern Cities without change. Passengers en route to or from Pensacola have no change of cars via this line between Cincinnati and Pensacola (Junction.)

Through Sleepers from Atlanta, Chattanooga, Little Rock, Memphis and Vicksburg make direct connection at Short Line Junction with Through Sleepers to New York and other Eastern Cities.

This is the only line running its entire trains from Louisville to Cincinnati and vice versa thereby causing no delay to Passengers (incident to other lines) by having to wait at Junctional Stations for delayed trains from other points in order to proceed to their destination.

It is Stone Ballasted, has a smooth track, and is entirely free from dust.

Tickets can be purchased via this line at all Ticket Offices in the North, East and South. Ask for Tickets via the Louisville and Cincinnati Short Line., (L., C. & L. R. R.)

S. S. PARKER, Gen'l P. & T. A.   JOHN MAC LEOD, Gen'l Sup't.

JOHN KILKENY, Gen'l Traveling Passenger Agent.

For a Copy of this Book Free send your address to W. D. CHIPLEY, Gen'l Manager P.R.R., Pensacola, Fla.